A DINOS FOR WASHINGTON

The True Story of Suciasaurus

Kelly Milner Halls

With illustrations by
Rick Spears

little bigfoot
an imprint of sasquatch books
seattle, wa

A cool breeze blew over the Pacific Ocean as fossil hunters Jim Goedert and David Starr landed on the waters of the San Juan Islands of Washington State in May 2010. Waves slapped against their seaplane as it sputtered toward Fossil Bay, a cove within the Sucia Island Marine State Park.

Sucia Island is home to one of the only known sources of Cretaceous strata—rocks from the days of the dinosaurs.

Jim Goedert and David Starr flew a seaplane to Sucia Island, one of the San Juan Islands off the coast of Washington State, in the Pacific Ocean.

Dinosaurs roamed the earth during most of the Mesozoic era—
252 million to 66 million years ago. The Mesozoic era is divided
into three subsets called periods. The first and oldest period is
called the Triassic. The second is the Jurassic. And the last and
youngest is the Cretaceous.

THE MESOZOIC ERA

66
Million
Years Ago

Cretaceous *Tyrannosaurus*

145
Million
Years Ago

Jurassic *Allosaurus*

199
Million
Years Ago

Triassic *Coelophysis*

252
Million
Years Ago

Washington State was under water during most of the Mesozoic era, so Fossil Bay is a rare treasure trove of marine fossils. Jim and David often searched there for prehistoric ammonites—spiral-shelled mollusks that once thrived in the shallow ocean.

Dazzling marine animal fossils were often revealed by erosion—the removal of soil and rock by pounding, powerful ocean waves and rainstorms—on the face of rocky walls or scattered across the beach. So Jim hiked the cliffs as David raked the gravel on the shore.

Ammonites, like this one, are plentiful in Sucia Island's Fossil Bay.

Living ammonite

Once found, fossils on public lands like state or national parks belong to all American citizens—every single one of us. Natural resources found on public lands also belong to us, but only people with written permission, called permits, are allowed to collect fossils in places like Sucia Island.

Jim and David were granted a permit because they promised to give important fossils to the Burke Museum—an official repository or storage place—in Seattle, Washington. They could keep common fossils like ammonites.

The beach at Fossil Bay on Sucia Island.

The quest for fossil treasure is often a slow process. Eyes are glued to the ground and to huge stones or towering cliffs called rocky outcrops. Feet shuffle cautiously, sometimes only inches at a time. It's like finding a needle in a haystack—a tiny gem more than 65 million years in the making.

Jim didn't expect to find anything important, so when he found a rare treasure, he rushed back to David on the beach, bursting with excitement. "Look at this!" he said. Resting in the curve of his fingers was a softball-sized piece of fossilized bone. Jim had a feeling they might find even more.

They spent the rest of the day searching, without finding more of the ancient bone. But they were not willing to give up—yet.

Finding fossils in the gravel requires focus. How many can you find?
Turn to the last page of the book to see how many you found.

Fossil hunters like Jim and David say the search is like prospecting for gold. When you find one real treasure, you go back until you find more, even if it takes years. So they flew back to Fossil Bay in April 2011 and again in March 2012. On that third trip, their patience paid off big time!

At the base of a cliff, in plain sight, was an even bigger piece of fossilized bone. The two pieces—the first one Jim found in 2010 and the one still locked in stone on the beach—fit together, like a hand in a glove.

What had they discovered? David had a collection of fossilized crabs, so he knew the fossilized bone was too big to be a crab.

Jim Goedert snapped a picture of the rare fossil he found on Sucia Island, the first of the two fossils discovered that fit together to make up Washington's first dinosaur fossil.

Prehistoric whale

Jim collected large, prehistoric whale bones. But whales didn't exist in the dinosaur age.

To solve the mystery, Jim and David needed expert help and special excavation tools, so they reached out to the dinosaur scientists at the Burke Museum.

Fossilized crab

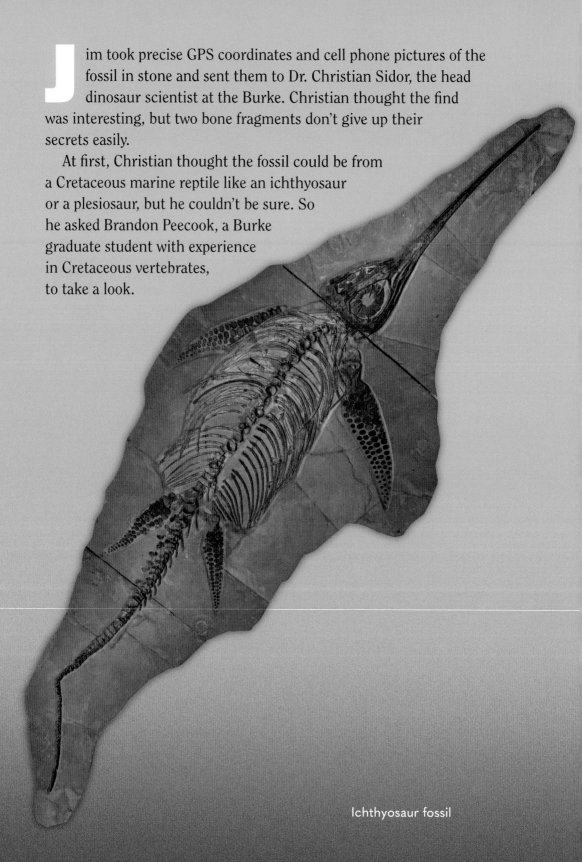

Jim took precise GPS coordinates and cell phone pictures of the fossil in stone and sent them to Dr. Christian Sidor, the head dinosaur scientist at the Burke. Christian thought the find was interesting, but two bone fragments don't give up their secrets easily.

At first, Christian thought the fossil could be from a Cretaceous marine reptile like an ichthyosaur or a plesiosaur, but he couldn't be sure. So he asked Brandon Peecook, a Burke graduate student with experience in Cretaceous vertebrates, to take a look.

Ichthyosaur fossil

Brandon was super excited. He wanted to head to Fossil Bay right away to rescue the bone. He wanted to study it closely. But it took a month to gather the people and the necessary equipment to free the fossil.

Finally, in April 2012, Brandon and a team from the Burke were on their way to the location Jim had mapped out on Sucia Island. This time the fossil hunters traveled by boat.

Living ichthyosaur

When the tide was out on Fossil Bay, many fossils were within reach.
But when the tide came in, they could disappear.

Brandon found the bone locked in a bed of mudstone, a concrete-like rock that is difficult to chip out of the ground. So he had to use a diamond blade saw.

Like a sculptor, he cut and carved for nearly four hours to free the fossil and the slab of stone that had protected it for approximately 80 million years.

Slicing through the stone wasn't the hardest part of the job. Fighting the rising tides was the team's biggest challenge. The bone was visible when the tide was out, but hidden under water when the tide came back in. That kept it hidden for centuries. The Burke team had to work as quickly as possible to claim their treasure, and they were thrilled when they did.

Little did they know how important it was to succeed when they did. Just a few days later, a landslide covered the spot where the bone had been discovered and left a deep layer of dirt and stone. If the scientists had waited even one week longer to mount their search, the fossil would have been lost forever.

Brandon was sure the fossil was special. Christian knew he might be right, but the fossil didn't look very promising at first. It was covered in stone and barnacles. Until they could clean it up, they wouldn't know for sure.

Millions of years of erosion—crashing waves wearing down and washing away layers of rock—revealed the dinosaur bone.

Fossil preparation at the Burke Museum.

The Burke's head of fossil preparation, Bruce Crowley, stepped in to make that happen. He and specially trained museum volunteer Donna Ritchie started the slow process of chipping mudstone away from fossilized bone. It wasn't pretty—yet. But Bruce knew a large piece of bone from Sucia Island could be something big.

Using pneumatic—air powered—hammers and drills, Bruce removed the biggest chunks of rock from the bone. He then turned to more delicate drills to protect the fossil. With the help of a high-powered microscope, Bruce could finish cleaning the bone without damaging it. Once it was prepared, the fossil could whisper its secrets.

It took Bruce and Donna almost two years to complete the job, but the results were sensational. The pieces of bone were well preserved and full of biological clues—clues that might help them identify what animal had been fossilized.

What were some of them?

Christian noticed there was a deep ridge—a scar on the bone where a muscle would have been attached when the animal was alive. That deep scar meant the animal was once strong and powerful. That clue might help identify the fossil.

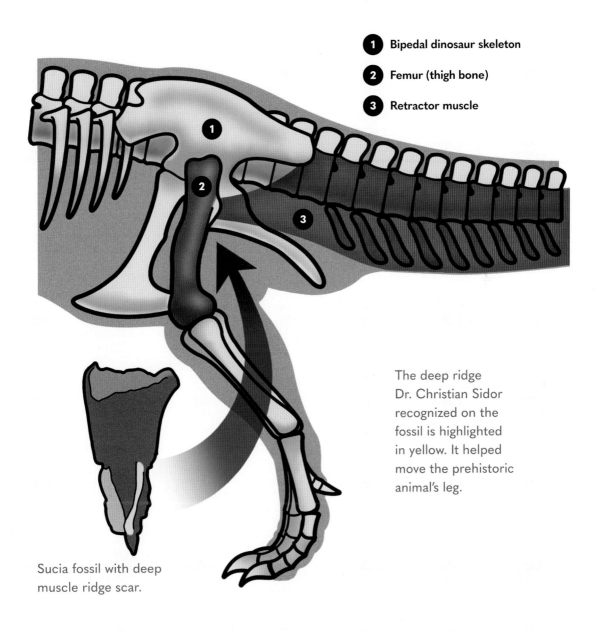

1 Bipedal dinosaur skeleton

2 Femur (thigh bone)

3 Retractor muscle

The deep ridge Dr. Christian Sidor recognized on the fossil is highlighted in yellow. It helped move the prehistoric animal's leg.

Sucia fossil with deep muscle ridge scar.

The size of the bone offered more clues—together the two pieces weighed about fifteen pounds and were 16.7 inches long and 8.7 inches wide. It was clear that the fossil was incomplete and had once belonged to a much larger bone. It was too big to belong to a marine reptile that thrived when Washington was under a prehistoric sea.

That gave Christian and Brandon a new direction to go in search of clues. If the fossil was too big to be a part of a marine reptile, it had to be part of a dinosaur, which can only be land dwelling.

Dr. Christian Sidor holds the Washington dinosaur fossil (left) and Dr. Brandon Peecook holds a cast of a Daspletosaurus femur, which they used to help determine if the Washington dinosaur fossil may have been part of a larger dinosaur leg bone.

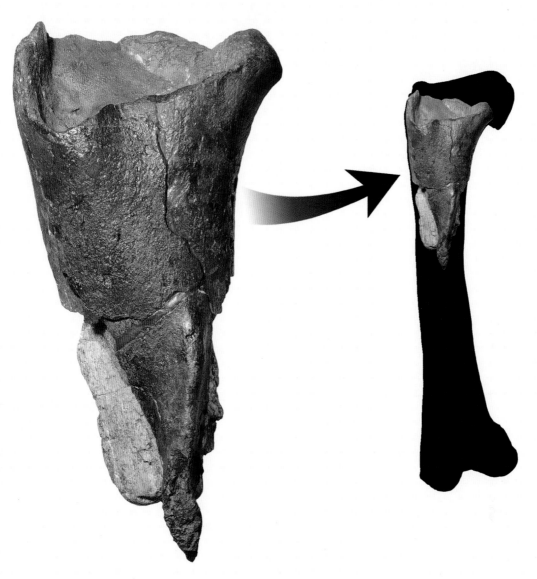

Washington dinosaur fossil fragment after it's been cleaned and repaired by adhering the two pieces together.

How did the fossil fragment fit into a whole, once living animal? Answering that question was like putting together a jigsaw puzzle without a picture to guide the scientists.

The Burke now had the only dinosaur bone ever unearthed in the Evergreen State. It was, literally, one of a kind. It made Washington State the thirty-seventh state to unearth a dinosaur fossil. Learning more would require a lot of questions, and questions are the heart of expanding scientific knowledge.

Which dinosaur was it from? Could it be from the same dinosaur species found in nearby Oregon—a region that was also under water at the time?

A dinosaur toe bone and a vertebra—part of a dinosaur's backbone—was discovered in Oregon. Both of the Oregon fossils were from a plant-eating dinosaur similar to an iguanodon.

They determined that the Burke fossilized bone was too big to be part of an iguanodon, but both the Oregon and Burke dinosaurs probably met the same fate. Learning about how they died could be another piece of the puzzle.

Both animals had been found nestled among the shells of a prehistoric ocean. How did they wind up there? Greg said it was probably a matter of "bloat and float."

If a dinosaur died on shore and was washed out to sea, the body could fill with gases and bloat like a balloon. Once the gas inside caused the carcass to split open, it could sink and fossilize.

These dinosaur toe bones were found in Oregon by paleontology professor Gregg Retallack. They were identified as potentially belonging to a dinosaur such as an iguanodon, which may have met a similar death as the mystery Washington dinosaur.

Living iguanodons

Why were so few of the fossilized remains found? Prehistoric sharks and mosasaurs might have been why. They didn't watch rotting bodies float by. They ate them. If a group of predators gathered, a feeding frenzy could erupt. A toe bone and a vertebra could drift down to the sandy bottom of the sea unnoticed, to be preserved for millions of years.

Did the Burke's dinosaur die the same way? It's possible. But regardless of how it died, the scientists determined the dinosaur had hollow bones filled with tiny sea creatures—hollow like the bones of other theropods, called tyrannosaurs, like a meat-eating *Tyrannosaurus rex* or an *Allosaurus*. This was probably a mystery theropod—a three-toed meat-eating dinosaur.

The Burke Museum had part of a theropod, but which part was it? Some of the best paleontologists in North America were enlisted to help find out. The theories they shared were exciting.

Clam fossils like these were found inside the Washington State dinosaur fossil. That meant the bone was hollow.

Mosasaurs eating a tyrannosaur's lifeless body.

Dr. Philip Currie of the Royal Tyrrell Museum in Alberta, Canada, was one of the first to examine the fossil.

He found it very interesting and felt it did not need to be complete to be important. When dinosaur fossils are rare, as they are on the Pacific coast, every scrap can help us understand the past.

Philip agreed it was a theropod—probably a tyrannosaur limb bone. At first, Christian and Brandon wondered if it was part of a tibia—the large bone of the lower leg. But after visiting the Royal Tyrrell Museum and examining other theropod bones, they concluded the bone was the upper portion of a femur, which is the thigh.

Dr. Philip Currie, one of Canada's foremost authorities on theropods, helped solve the dinosaur mystery.

Skull of *Daspletosaurus*, a close relative of *Tyrannosaurus*.

The complete bone would have been about three feet long. It was too short to be from *Tyrannosaurus rex*, which had a four-foot femur. But it was a big theropod, between twenty and twenty-five feet long. It was a nice match in size to the femur of *Daspletosaurus*—a relative of the *T. rex* that lived between 86 and 66 million years ago. Now that more clues were being unveiled, it was time to find a theropod expert.

Famed Montana paleontologist Dr. Jack Horner knows all about theropods. He has collected twelve *T. rex* specimens and brought them back to the Museum of the Rockies—a repository like the Burke—at Montana State University in Bozeman.

Jack agreed that the fossil had to be a theropod and that it could be part of a *Daspletosaurus*.

How a big dinosaur like a *Daspletosaurus* wound up on an island in the Pacific Ocean was the next question.

One theory—an older theory—suggests the fossil was found on an island off the coast of Washington because of shifting of underground tectonic plates. Billions of years ago, there was only one supercontinent. It was called Pangaea. The rumbling of these underground plates shattered Pangaea into the landmasses we know today: Africa, Antarctica, Eurasia, Australia, North America, and South America.

Perhaps a piece of land that what was once near Mexico drifted all the way to the Pacific Northwest to become Sucia Island. If so, Washington's mystery theropod may have died nearly 2,700 miles south of its final resting place.

Dr. Jack Horner has collected dozens of tyrannosaur fossils.

Eurasia

North
America

Africa

South
America

India

Antarctica

Australia

**Region from
where Sucia
Island may have
originated.**

Washington's dinosaur fossil may have slid north with the shifting of
tectonic plates.

The second theory is the fossil might have come from Methow
Valley, a place roughly 200 miles northeast of Seattle that also has
Cretaceous rock.

But how did a dinosaur that lived that far from the coast wind
up on Sucia Island? Jack says it might have fallen into a raging
river, drowned, and traveled all the way to the Pacific Ocean from
the valley.

Washington State's Methow Valley has Cretaceous rocks that are protected by plant life.

I
f the Burke theropod lived and died in Methow Valley and that area has Cretaceous rock, why haven't scientists found dinosaur fossils there? The answer is vegetation.

In places like South Dakota, Montana, and Wyoming where dinosaur fossils are found, there is very little vegetation to hold the rocks together. The rain and wind break the rocks apart, and the fossils can be seen in the eroded gravel. Those dry dinosaur beds are often called the Badlands.

Methow Valley is not like the Badlands. It is covered in thick, lush trees and grasses. The vegetation's root system holds even broken rocks together. The fossils never wash down the hillsides the way they do in the Badlands. In Methow Valley, they remain safely hidden away.

Does Christian agree with Jack's Methow Valley hypothesis? He agrees it is possible. But we may never know where the theropod bone actually came from.

In the South Dakota Badlands, where there is less vegetation, fossils are more easily exposed by erosion.

Most fossilized bones are found once erosion washes away the rock that has kept them safe for millions of years. Paleontologists search for exposed bone in places carved by wind and weather.

Until scientists gather more facts, we won't know for sure which theropod wound up on Sucia Island. Philip thinks finding more clues is possible. He thinks if one fossil was discovered, others could be waiting. But it won't be easy. If most of the dinosaur was eaten by prehistoric sea creatures, there may be nothing left to find.

For now, we'll have to be satisfied with the theropod leg exhibit at the Burke Museum, which scientists nicknamed Suciasaurus after the island where it was found. Gazing at that treasure of a thigh bone makes it easy to hope that if there is more to unearth, it will be found by fossil hunters yet to come.

Perhaps that fossil hunter could be you!

Theoretical life restoration of Suciasaurus.

TYRANNOSAUR FAMILY TREE

Many different kinds of dinosaurs once walked the earth. Each had its own family tree. Theropods, like tyrannosaurs, had a similar look, but key physical differences made the different species. These are a few of those tyrannosaurs, including Suciasaurus—Washington's only dinosaur discovery, so far.

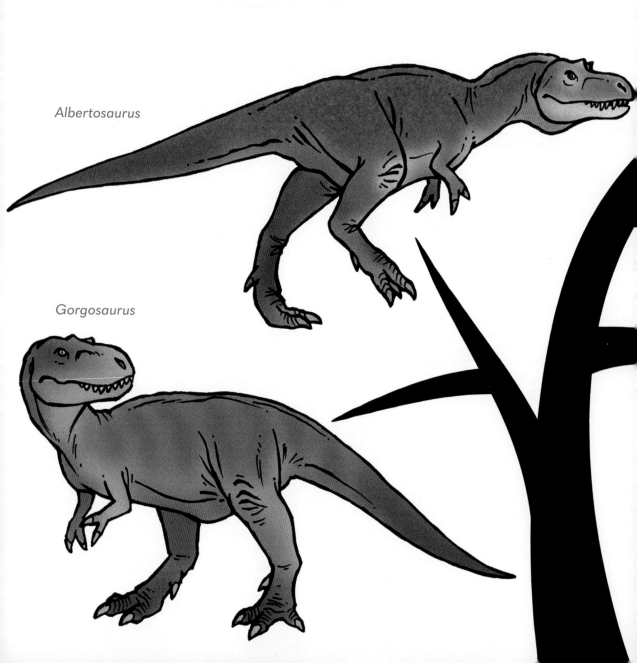

Albertosaurus

Gorgosaurus

Tyrannosaurus

Daspletosaurus

Suciasaurus

NAME THAT THEROPOD

Does Washington State's mystery theropod have a name? Not exactly. Normally, the person who discovers a new dinosaur species gets to name it. But there is no way to know if this is a new theropod or an old favorite, such as *Daspletosaurus*. So, for now, it's referred to by its specimen number UWBM 95770. The team at the Burke gave it a nickname, Suciasaurus, for the island where it was unearthed.

WASHINGTON'S STATE DINOSAUR, BY LAW?

When fourth graders at Elmhurst Elementary in Tacoma, Washington, discovered some American states had official dinosaurs, they wrote to State Representative Melanie Morgan, asking if she'd help make Suciasaurus their official dinosaur.

"The Burke Museum in Seattle showcases the fossil and even advertises the Suciasaurus on museum merchandise," they wrote. "We think this evidence shows [it] should be our state dinosaur."

Rep. Morgan agreed. It took four years, but in April of 2023, House Bill 2155 became law and Governor Jay Inslee's signature made it official. That's proof—kids can make a difference, when they make their voices heard.

Washington State Governor Jay Inslee signs the bill into law, making Suciasaurus the official state fossil.

FOSSIL HUNTING? BE PREPARED!

If you're hoping to look for fossils, you'll need to be prepared for success. Here are a few tips on what you should bring into the field in your backpack.

Clothing

Wear warm clothes in the cool mornings, but pack lighter clothes for later in the day. Rugged sneakers or boots are the best options for shoes.

Medical Supplies

Pack bug spray, sunscreen, and a small first aid kit for cuts and scrapes.

Food

Some fossil hunts take hours, so pack plenty of food and water just to be safe.

Tools

SMALL HAMMER: For breaking rocks into smaller pieces.

SMALL CHISEL: For chipping away layers of rock to see what's in between.

PAINTBRUSH: Once you've found a fossil, a paintbrush will help sweep dirt and sand away from your fossil without damaging it.

PLASTIC BAGS THAT SEAL: Plastic bags are a safe place to store your fossil until you get home. Mark the bag with the date, time, and location of the discovery.

PERMANENT MARKER: To take notes in your notebook and to label your plastic bags.

CELL PHONE OR CAMERA: Take pictures of your dig sites and GPS coordinates.

NOTEBOOK: Record your GPS coordinates to track where you found your fossil so you can go back to the same spot or so you can tell paleontologists where you found your fossil. They may want to prospect for fossils there too.

FOSSIL PREPARATION TOOLS

Museums have special labs to prepare fossils still encased in stone. These are a few of the items found in those labs.

PROTECTIVE MASKS AND GOGGLES: Keep rock chips from hurting eyes.

GLOVES: Worn to protect skin from chemicals and glues.

EARPLUGS: When using power drills, protection from sound can be important.

PNEUMATIC HAMMERS AND DRILLS: Fine-pointed needles and chisels are powered by air to help chip away the rock.

DENTAL TOOLS AND DRILLS: Once most of the rock is removed from fossils, smaller tools are used to protect the fragile bone pieces.

BRUSHES: Brushes remove dust from bone without harming the bone.

SPECIMEN TRAYS: Trays help keep fossils safe after they're removed from rock.

GLUES AND ADHESIVES: If a fossil is broken, and most are, glue keeps them from falling apart.

MICROSCOPES: If fossils are tiny, microscopes make it easier to free them from rock.

DUST VACUUMS: Dust can damage the tools used in preparation and the lungs of people who do the job. Vacuum systems keep the dust in check.

OFFICIAL STATE DINOSAURS

COLORADO: *Stegosaurus*, an armored dinosaur

MARYLAND: *Astrodon*, a sauropod

MISSOURI: *Hypsibema*, a hadrosaur

NEW JERSEY: *Hadrosaurus*, a hadrosaur

OKLAHOMA: *Acrocanthosaurus*, a theropod

WYOMING: *Triceratops*, a horned dinosaur

TEXAS: *Paluxysaurus*, a sauropod

WASHINGTON: Suciasaurus (nickname), a tyrannosaur

WASHINGTON, D.C.: *Capitalsaurus*, a theropod

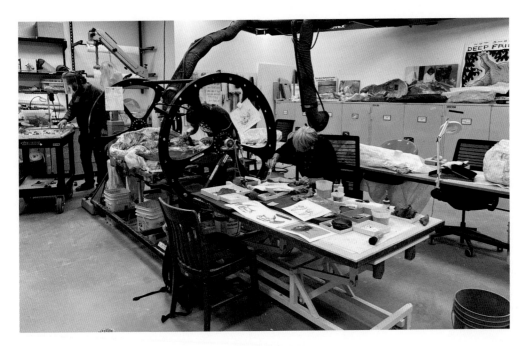

Fossil preparation unfolds in the Burke lab.

LEARN MORE ABOUT IT

These books, videos, and websites are a great place to start.

Books

Dinosaur Lady: The Daring Discoveries of Mary Anning, the First Paleontologist,
   by Linda Skeers and Marta Álvarez Miguéns (2020)
When Sue Found Sue: Sue Hendrickson Discovers Her T. Rex, by Toni Buzzeo (2019)
Fossil Huntress: Mary Leakey, Paleontologist, by Andi Diehn (2019)
***Fossils for Kids: A Junior Scientist's Guide to Dinosaur Bones, Ancient Animals, and
   Prehistoric Life on Earth***, by Ashley Hall (2020)

Videos

Dig into Paleontology—SciShow Kids
Youtube.com/watch?v=1FjyKmpmQzc

Fossils for Kids—Learn Bright
Youtube.com/watch?v=QPIDE_VWxsI

How Do Dinosaur Fossils Form—Natural History Museum
Youtube.com/watch?v=87E8bQrX4Wg

Generation Genius: Fossils and Extinction (3rd, 4th, 5th graders)
GenerationGenius.com/videolessons/fossils-and-extinction-video-for-kids

Generation Genius: The Fossil Record (6th, 7th, 8th graders)
GenerationGenius.com/videolessons/fossil-record-video-for-kids

Websites

Fossil Facts for Kids/DK Find Out!
DKFindout.com/us/dinosaurs-and-prehistoric-life/fossils

Paleontology for Kids/American Museum of Natural History's OLogy
Amnh.org/explore/ology/paleontology

Explaining Fossils for Kids/Love to Know
Kids.LovetoKnow.com/childrens-education/explaining-fossils-kids

Fossils for Kids
FossilsforKids.com

Places to Dig

Republic, Washington—Stonerose Interpretive Center
Stonerosefossil.org

Fossil, Oregon—Wheeler High School Dig Site
OregonPaleolandscenter.com/wheeler-high-school-fossil-beds

Billings, Montana—Judith River Dinosaur Institute
MontanaDinosaurdigs.com

Ekalaka, Montana—Carter County Museum
CarterCountyMuseum.org

Casper, Wyoming—Tate Geological Museum at Casper College
CasperCollege.edu/tate-geological-museum

Thermopolis, Wyoming—Wyoming Dinosaur Center
WyomingDinosaurCenter.org

Fruita, Colorado—Museums of Western Colorado/Dinosaur Journey
MuseumofWesternco.com/visit/dinosaur-journey

ABOUT THE BURKE MUSEUM

Founded in 1885, the Burke Museum, located on the University of Washington's original campus in downtown Seattle, is the oldest public museum in Washington State and was named the state museum of natural history and culture in 1899. In the decades since, the museum has collected more than 18 million objects reflective of the unique history of the Evergreen State.

Thousands of public school students visit the museum every year, where they can see the only real dinosaur fossils on display in the state, including Suciasaurus, and watch paleontologists remove rock from newly discovered fossils.

Suciasaurus studies its own fossil.

GLOSSARY

AMMONITE: Prehistoric shelled creature closely related to modern cephalopods, such as octopus, squid, and cuttlefish

ANATOMICAL: Related to the anatomy or physical structure of a living creature

BARNACLE: A shellfish related to crabs and lobsters that live in ocean waters

BIODIVERSITY: The vast collection of life on earth

BIPEDAL: Animal species that walks on two feet

DIAGNOSTIC: Educated understanding of a species or physical function

ENCASEMENT: Material that surrounds or encases a separate object or animal

EXCAVATION: The process of removing scientific items from the rock or the soil

FRAGMENT: Broken pieces of a once whole object

GEOPHYSICIST: Scientist who studies the physical workings of planet Earth

GPS: Satellite navigation system used to mark or find locations

HADROSAUR: Plant-eating dinosaur with a bill-shaped mouth

ICHTHYOSAUR: Extinct marine reptile with a long snout

IGUANODON: Species of plant-eating dinosaur, related to hadrosaur

INVERTEBRATE: Animal species without a spinal cord/backbone

LIMESTONE: Rock made up of crushed organic materials, including shells and corals

MATRIX: Rock that encases a fossil

MOSASAUR: Huge, fish-eating prehistoric marine reptile possibly related to modern day monitor lizards

ORNITHOPOD: Another term for hadrosaur, bipedal plant-eating dinosaur

PALEONTOLOGIST: A scientist that studies prehistoric life

PANGAEA: Supercontinent of most of the world's seven known land masses before they broke apart and drifted to their current locations

PAYDIRT: Earth or stone that yields a valuable object

PERMIT: Paper that grants official permission to take some kind of action

PLESIOSAUR: Long-necked, meat-eating prehistoric marine reptile with flippers

PNEUMATIC TOOL: Uses compressed air to function

PREHISTORIC: Events that happened before people began to record historic events on paper

PREPARATOR: Person who carefully removes the matrix from a fossil for museum display

REPOSITORY: Place or institution charged with storing and caring for fossils collected on federal lands

SAUROPOD: Plant-eating, long-necked dinosaur that walked on four legs (quadruped)

SEDIMENTARY: Rock formed by layers of sediment

SPECIMEN: Individual plant, rock, or animal collected for study

SPECIMEN NUMBER: Unique number given to found objects and used for tracking

SPIRAL: Coiled or curved object or formation

STRATA: Layers of compressed dirt that can be rock or compressed dirt that is almost rock

SUBSURFACE: Under the surface

TECTONIC: Strong or widespread impact

TERRESTRIAL: Relating to the earth

THEROPOD: Bipedal, meat-eating dinosaur like *Tyrannosaurus rex* or *Allosaurus*

VERTEBRATE: An animal with a spine or backbone

Sauropod

This book is dedicated to Jim Goedert, David Starr, Dr. Christian Sidor, Dr. Brendan Peecook, Kelsie Abrams, Dr. Jack Horner, and Dr. Philip Currie who helped us pull all this information together. Thank you so much. –KMH

To awesome fossil preparators everywhere whose skills bring our view of the prehistoric past into sharper focus. Thank you! –RS

Printed in China by Dream Colour Printing Ltd. in April 2024

LITTLE BIGFOOT with colophon is a registered trademark of Penguin Random House LLC

28 27 26 25 24   9 8 7 6 5 4 3 2 1

Editor: Christy Cox
Production editor: Peggy Gannon
Designer: Tony Ong
Cover illustration: Rick Spears
Interior illustrations: Rick Spears

Interior photographs:
Seaplane photo (page 2): © Jim Goedert
Sucia Island photo (page 2): © Christopher S. Teren
Ammonite photo (page 4): © Alex Sidles
Fossil Bay beach photo (page 6): © Burke Museum
Fossils in gravel photo (pages 7 & 40): © Taylor L. Brown
First piece of fossil photo (page 8): © Jim Goedert
Ichthyosaur photo (page 10): © Rob Casey
Fossil Bay photo (page 12): © Hobbes Barber
Fossil prep photo (page 14): © Burke Museum
Paleontologists with fossil photo (page 16): © Burke Museum
Toe bones photo (page 18): © Gregg Retallack
Prehistoric Clams (page 20): © Adobe/PKZ
Dr. Philip Currie photo (page 22): © Eva Koppelthus
Paleontologist Jack Horner photo (page 24): © Jack Horner
Methow Valley photo (page 26): © David Lukas
Badlands photo (page 27): © Louie Psihoyos
Governor Inslee signing bill photo (page 32): © Gov. Inslee
Fossil prep photo (page 35): © Burke Museum

Library of Congress Cataloging-in-Publication Data is available.

ISBN: 978-1-63217-456-7 (Hardcover)
ISBN: 978-1-63217-562-5 (Paperback)

Sasquatch Books
1325 Fourth Avenue, Suite 1025
Seattle, WA 98101

SasquatchBooks.com

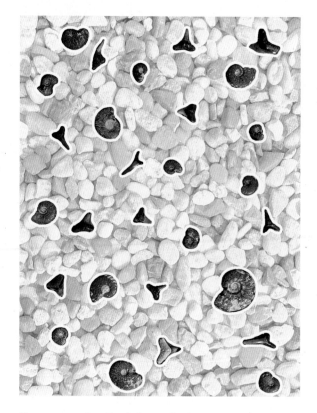

How many fossils did you find on page 7?

FSC
www.fsc.org

MIX
Paper from
responsible sources
FSC® C188448